J 551.6 Roy
Royston, Angela
The race
change

$30.25
ocn890118108
First edition.   07/17/2015

## WORLD IN CRISIS

# THE RACE TO SURVIVE
# CLIMATE CHANGE

### Angela Royston

NEW YORK

Published in 2015 by The Rosen Publishing Group, Inc.
29 East 21st Street
New York, NY 10010

Copyright © 2015 by The Rosen Publishing Group, Inc.

First Edition

All rights reserved. No part of this book may be reproduced in any form without permission in writing from the publisher, except by a reviewer.

Produced for Rosen by Calcium Creative Ltd.
Editor for Calcium Creative Ltd.: Sarah Eason
Designer: Paul Myerscough
Picture research: Rachel Blount

**Library of Congress Cataloging-in-Publication Data**

Royston, Angela.
The race to survive climate change/by Angela Royston, first edition.
    p. cm.—(World in crisis)
Includes bibliographical references and index.
ISBN 978-1-4777-7-848-7 (library binding)
1. Climatic changes—Juvenile literature. 2. Global warming—Juvenile literature. 3. Nature—Effect of human beings on—Juvenile literature.
I. Royston, Angela, 1945–. II. Title.
QC981.8.C5 R69 2015
551.6—d23

*Manufactured in Malaysia*

Photo credits: Cover: Shutterstock: Lee Prince; Inside: Dreamstime: Awcnz62 41, Ricardo Esplana Babor 45, Bernard Breton 26, Chriswood44 27, Cpenler 43, Editor77 39, David Gaylor 31, Moose Henderson 22, Shawn Jackson 25, Marcelmooij 34, Nitsuki 44, Phfw22 9, Roza 38, Smellme 23, Staphy 28, Tebnad 40, Tonyv3112 37, Shao-chun Wang 36, Robert Zehetmayer 32; NASA: Goddard Space Flight Center 12; Shutterstock: ArtisticPhoto 8, Brisbane 13, Tony Campbell 18, Ethan Daniels 24, Dirk Ercken 20, Frontpage 11, Markus Gann 6, Volodymyr Goinyk 7, GOLFX 17, Gouvi 10, Olivier Le Moal 42, Mikenorton 16, Sari ONeal 5, Nicram Sabod 29, Todd Shoemake 14, StacieStauffSmith Photos 15, Tntphototravis 21, VitaSerendipity 19, Leanne Vorrias 4, Christopher Wood 30; Wikimedia Commons: Davidarfonjones 33, Smiley.toerist 35.

# Contents

**Introduction**
The Race Is On　　　　　　　　　　　　4

**Chapter One**
The Problem　　　　　　　　　　　　　6

**Chapter Two**
Extreme and Unpredictable　　　　　　12

**Chapter Three**
Ecosystems in Turmoil　　　　　　　　20

**Chapter Four**
Melting Ice　　　　　　　　　　　　　28

**Chapter Five**
Cutting the Carbon　　　　　　　　　　36

Glossary　　　　　　　　　　　　　　46
Further Reading　　　　　　　　　　　47
Index　　　　　　　　　　　　　　　　48

# INTRODUCTION

# The Race Is On

The race against climate change is a race for survival. At stake are the futures of millions, or perhaps billions, of people and the extinction of many species of animals and plants. The cause of these possible catastrophes is a small rise in the average temperature of the surface of Earth.

## Monitoring Climate Change

Weather stations, weather ships, and satellites in space collect information about the weather from places all over the world. They measure and record data such as air temperature, wind speed, and rainfall. For many years, scientists and government experts have been worried that Earth is becoming warmer. In 1988, the Intergovernmental Panel on Climate Change (IPCC) was set up to assess the evidence for, and predict the likely effects of, climate change.

## A Panel of Experts

Thousands of scientists work for the IPCC. They include many different types of scientific experts, including meteorologists and ecologists. Every few years, they report on the latest information about the weather and changes to the atmosphere. They also figure out how the average temperature of Earth has changed.

People love lying on hot sands and swimming in warm seas. Some places, however, such as the Mediterranean, could soon be too hot for vacations.

# THE RACE IS ON

## Scientific Predictions

According to NASA's climate scientists, the average temperature at Earth's surface has increased by about 1.4° Fahrenheit (0.8° Celsius) since 1880. Two-thirds of the increase has occurred since 1975. A few degrees rise may sound unimportant, but it takes a lot of extra heat to raise the average temperature by just one degree. This book examines the causes and consequences of climate change, such as extreme weather and rising sea levels, and what we can do about it.

### LOOK TO THE PAST

Earth has warmed and cooled in the past. About 650,000 years ago, the average temperature was cooler by about 9°F (5°C). All year round, thick ice more than 1 mile (1.6 kilometers) deep covered much of the Northern Hemisphere. In North America it reached as far south as the Midwest.

The number of monarch butterflies that migrate to Mexico for the winter has dropped alarmingly. The World Wildlife Fund (WWF) says this is partly due to climate change.

CHAPTER ONE

# The Problem

In 2005, the IPCC reported that the average temperature of Earth had risen by 1.4°F (0.8°C) in the past 100 years. This is called global warming. Although Earth has warmed and cooled in the past, the temperature has never changed so quickly. In the last ice age, it took 10,000 years for Earth to warm by 9°F (5°C). If temperatures on Earth continue to rise at their current rate, we may warm by that amount in less than 100 years.

## What Makes Earth Warm?

Heat from the sun warms the surface of Earth during the day. Some of the heat is reflected straight back into space, but some is absorbed and then released. Clouds of water vapor trap the released heat. The clouds act like a blanket that helps keep us warm at night.

The sun radiates a huge amount of energy, which reaches us as light and heat. The temperature at its surface is about 10,000°F (5,500°C).

# THE PROBLEM

> In summer, Antarctica becomes warmer and some of the ice melts. Large chunks of ice break off the thick ice sheet that covers the land and slide into the sea.

## Greenhouse Gases

Water vapor is one of several gases in the air that trap the sun's heat. They are called greenhouse gases because, just as a greenhouse generates warmth for plants, the gases keep Earth warmer than it otherwise would be. Other than water vapor, the most common greenhouse gas is carbon dioxide, although the less common gas methane has an even more powerful warming effect.

## Long-Term Effects

Scientists on various research stations in the Antarctic have studied ice cores there to measure the amount of greenhouse gases in the air in the past. They have found that when carbon dioxide and methane in the air increase, Earth becomes warmer. When greenhouse gases in the air reduce, Earth cools down. It takes time for the effects of greenhouse gases to be felt on Earth. Gases emitted today will not begin to affect temperatures for several years.

### COUNTDOWN!

In 2013, the IPCC warned that, if we do not drastically limit the emission of further carbon dioxide, Earth's temperature could rise by as much as 8.1°F (4.5°C) by 2100. The IPCC urged that we do everything we can to limit the rise to 3.6°F (2°C).

# THE RACE TO SURVIVE CLIMATE CHANGE

Wires carry electricity across the country. We need electricity, but the way most of it is generated is endangering the planet.

## Why Is This Happening Now?

In 2013, the IPCC reported that the rise in Earth's average temperature was almost certainly due to human activities. Since the Industrial Revolution began in the eighteenth century, humans have produced more and more greenhouse gases, mainly by burning fossil fuels, the most common of which are coal, oil, and natural gas.

## The Industrial Revolution

Before the late eighteenth century, people used wind, running water, or animals to power their machines. Around 1764, the Scottish engineer James Watt invented a new, more efficient way to burn coal to make steam to drive an engine. As a result, industry and transportation were transformed. Using Watt's steam engine, factories manufactured enormous quantities of cheap goods, and by the mid-nineteenth century people could travel by steam train. Toward the end of the nineteenth century, engineers developed ways of using steam power to generate electricity.

# THE PROBLEM

## The High Cost of Better Lives

The Industrial Revolution and the inventions that followed it revolutionized people's lives. Inventions included automobiles and aircraft, which burn fuel made from oil, and electrical machines, such as telephones and computers. Our lives today are easier and more comfortable than they were hundreds of years ago. However, our improved lifestyles rely on burning the fossil fuels coal, oil, and natural gas that are the cause of today's climate change problem.

## A Burning Issue

Fossil fuels consist mostly of carbon. When they burn, the carbon combines with oxygen to form carbon dioxide. Since the Industrial Revolution, people have burned more and more fossil fuel. In doing so, they have produced trillions of tons of carbon dioxide, most of which is now trapped in Earth's atmosphere.

▲ Aircraft are convenient for long journeys, but they burn more fuel than other ways of traveling and further add to global warming.

## SCIENCE SOLUTIONS

### Measuring Greenhouse Gas

Scientists have measured different greenhouse gases and compared their effects on climate change. According to the U.S. Environmental Protection Agency (EPA), carbon dioxide accounts for 84 percent of the United States' greenhouse gas emissions, while methane accounts for about 9 percent. However, the EPA says that the effect of 1 ton (0.9 metric tons) of methane on climate change is 25 times greater than the effect of the same amount of carbon dioxide.

# THE RACE TO SURVIVE CLIMATE CHANGE

## Out of Control?

As long as climate change is caused by human activities, we have the power to influence it. However, many scientists at the National Academy of Sciences now predict that some consequences of climate change can trigger global warming that is beyond our control. One such trigger, or "tipping point" as it is often called, is the melting of the Arctic tundra.

## Melting Permafrost

The Arctic tundra is an area of land just south of the North Pole. It is too cold for trees to grow there, and it is so cold that the ground beneath the surface stays frozen all year. This frozen ground is called permafrost. Climate change, however, is making the tundra warmer, and the permafrost is beginning to melt.

## Stores of Greenhouse Gas

The permafrost contains huge amounts of carbon dioxide, methane, and nitrous oxide. These greenhouse gases, formed over millions of years, are trapped in the frozen soil. As the tundra melts, the gases escape into the air. There, they increase global warming, which in turn causes more tundra to melt.

Moose graze on moss and other plants that grow on the tundra in summer, when the ice that usually covers the surface has melted.

# THE PROBLEM

Trees absorb carbon dioxide through their leaves and help to combat climate change. However, forests are being cut down for farming and mining minerals.

## Other Triggers

Additional climate change triggers include the melting of sea ice and the destruction of forests. Large trees, particularly rain forest trees, lock up enormous amounts of carbon for hundreds of years. When they are cut down or burned, the carbon they hold escapes into the atmosphere as carbon dioxide. As temperatures rise, forests are drying out. This leads to devastating wildfires, which add to global warming.

## COUNTDOWN!

The New Economics Foundation (NEF) is a group of economists and ecologists who promote economic action that does not harm the planet. In 2008, the group examined the scientific evidence for climate change and declared that the world had until 2016 to prevent global warming from exceeding the IPCC's safe limit of 3.6°F (2°C) by 2100. They called their warning the "100 Months" campaign.

CHAPTER TWO

# Extreme and Unpredictable

Climate change is already happening. According to the IPCC, no part of the world is unaffected by global warming. One of the most immediate effects of global warming is the difference it makes to the weather. Hurricanes, tornadoes, droughts, and other extreme forms of weather are already becoming more severe and occurring more frequently. In addition, weather is becoming less predictable.

## What Is Climate?

Climate is the type of weather that usually occurs in a particular place at different times of the year. In the Midwest, for example, winters are usually very cold and the ground is covered with snow. The summer is usually very hot. In California, it is warm all year round.

▲ Satellites in space photograph and track the paths of severe storms. This hurricane is about to hit the Eastern Seaboard.

## How Is Climate Changing?

Climates around the world are changing. For example, in the coming decades, meteorologists expect that the Midwest will have more heat waves in summer and warmer winters. Ice will melt earlier in spring, and lakes and rivers will freeze later in fall. According to the science action group the Union of Concerned Scientists (UCS), heavy rainfall is already twice as frequent as it used to be, and rivers in Illinois, Iowa, and Missouri are more likely to flood.

**EXTREME AND UNPREDICTABLE**

## Forecasting the Weather

The National Weather Service provides weather forecasts for the entire United States. It prepares its forecasts from information collected by weather stations across the country and from satellites orbiting high above Earth in space. Changing climates, however, make it harder for meteorologists to accurately predict the weather more than a few days ahead.

### LOOK TO THE PAST

For centuries, people used natural signs, such as the color of the sky at sunrise and sunset, to predict the coming weather. Thomas Jefferson, a Founding Father of the United States, was one of the first people to make a scientific study of climate. For fifty years, from 1776, he kept a weather diary, in which he recorded the weather day by day.

Devastating floods have hit many countries. In 2011, Brisbane in Australia was inundated when the Brisbane River broke its banks.

13

# THE RACE TO SURVIVE CLIMATE CHANGE

## Storms Ahead!

According to the EPA, extreme weather such as storms and floods will become more severe in future. The fiercest storms are tornadoes. A tornado affects only a small area, but it has the strongest winds of any storm. Hurricanes can measure hundreds of miles across—they are the world's biggest storms.

## Tornadoes

A tornado is a strong wind that spins upward into the cloud, sucking up dust and objects from the ground below. The stronger the wind, the bigger the objects it lifts. A tornado usually forms under a thunderstorm. Each tornado may last only a few minutes, but warmer climates are producing increasingly powerful thunderstorms. They generate one tornado after another, leaving behind a trail of destruction, sometimes across several states. In April 2011, a series of 358 tornadoes ripped across states from Texas to New York and Canada, killing 324 people.

## Hurricanes

A hurricane is a storm that forms over warm ocean water near the equator. Warm, wet air rises above the water,

> Every year about 800 tornadoes form over the Great Plains, mostly in an area known as Tornado Alley. They cause the most damage when they hit towns.

14

# EXTREME AND UNPREDICTABLE

pulling in cooler air to take its place below. The warmer the air is, the faster it rises and the stronger the winds around it are. As the storm strengthens, it rotates. The strongest winds blow around the eye, a calm area at the center of the storm. Climate change is making the oceans warmer, which in turn is creating even more severe storms, such as Typhoon Haiyan, which hit the Philippines in 2013 with powerful winds gusting up to 235 miles per hour (378 kilometers per hour).

## Predicting the Path of a Storm

Hurricanes change strength as they pass over warmer and cooler water. They can also change direction, making it very difficult for meteorologists to predict exactly where a hurricane will hit land and how strong it will be when it makes landfall.

## SCIENCE SOLUTIONS

### Measuring Storms

Meteorologists at the National Oceanic and Atmospheric Association (NOAA) use robots to help them predict more accurately the path and strength of a hurricane. They use unmanned aircraft, called drones, to fly directly into the eye of a hurricane to measure its wind speeds. They also use unmanned submarines, called underwater gliders, to measure the temperature of the ocean in front of the storm.

Towns and cities that are likely to be hit by hurricanes plan ahead to protect residents. Evacuation routes are clearly signposted to direct people to safety.

# THE RACE TO SURVIVE CLIMATE CHANGE

Wildfires are most common when the grass is tinder dry in summer. Winds fan the flames as they rip through crops and forests.

## Rain: Too Little and Too Much

Plants, including farm crops, and animals need rainwater to survive—but they must have the right amount of water. A long period of too little rain produces a drought, while too much rain can cause floods. Climate change will make droughts and floods more likely and more severe.

## Droughts

The IPCC predicts that climate change will make dry places, such as the southwestern United States, even drier. Some farmers can irrigate their crops during dry weather, using water from rivers, lakes, and wells. However, if these stores of water run out, the crops die. Grasslands and forests also suffer from drought. When trees and grass dry out, they easily catch fire. Wildfires spread quickly, burning buildings, crops, forests, and everything in their path.

## Floods

As Earth becomes warmer, some parts of the world will begin to get more rain than they usually do. For example, as the sea becomes warmer, more water evaporates into the atmosphere. Increased water vapor means more rain. Climate change is likely to cause an increase in intense, heavy rainfall. Heavy rain soaks the land and runs off into streams, lakes, and rivers. As the water level rises, the banks of rivers may burst.

**EXTREME AND UNPREDICTABLE**

## Flood Damage

Floods can ruin crops and destroy roads, bridges, and homes. Intense rain may cause a flash flood—a sudden flood that can overwhelm and drown animals and people. A flash flood can occur almost anywhere, even in a desert.

People escape from rising floodwaters however they can. Rescuers use boats and helicopters to reach people who are trapped.

## COUNTDOWN!

The National Research Council (NRC) advises the U.S. government about the evidence and likely impact of climate change. It uses computer models to predict the effect of global warming on the likelihood of severe weather. The NRC reports that extreme rainstorms are likely to increase by 5 to 10 percent with every 1.8°F (1°C) rise in temperature. At the same time, forest fires in the western United States and Canada are likely to double or even quadruple for every 1.8°F (1°C) of warming.

17

# THE RACE TO SURVIVE CLIMATE CHANGE

## Problems for Farmers

Farmers rely on the weather to water and ripen their crops. Traditional weather patterns are now less reliable because of global warming, and farmers face even more difficult times ahead. If crops fail, the price of food goes up, making life increasingly difficult for people everywhere.

## Less Food

Wheat, rice, and other cereals are staple foods. This means that they are the main source of food for people around the world. Cereal plants need water to grow and to swell the grains, so droughts mean smaller plants and smaller grains. The amount a crop produces is called a yield. According to the NRC, the yields of wheat in the United States, Africa, and India will drop by 5 to 15 percent for every 1.8°F (1°C) rise that occurs in Earth's average world temperature.

◀ A drought can last for weeks, months, or even years. It doesn't take long for the leaves of plants to dry up and die. The grains of cereal crops shrivel up, too.

18

# EXTREME AND UNPREDICTABLE

## Pests and Diseases

As the world warms, pests and diseases thrive in places that were once too cold for them. For example, the U.S. Forest Service is struggling to combat an outbreak of bark beetles in western states, from Mexico to Alaska. Since the 1990s, winters have been warmer in these areas, allowing beetles to produce young much more quickly. According to the Forest Service, bark beetles wiped out 3 million acres (1.2 million hectares) of spruce forests in Alaska during the 1990s.

## Predicting the Unpredictable

One of the biggest problems for farmers is not being able to predict the weather. If farmers know that a summer will be unusually dry, they can plant crops that require less water. If they know that there will be a heat wave at a certain time, they can plan the best time to sow seed for new crops. Without that certain knowledge, farmers have to guess what the weather will be and so could make expensive mistakes.

Many insects, such as the Colorado potato beetle, attack particular crops. Some pests drink the sap from stems, others attack the fruit, or leaves.

## SCIENCE SOLUTIONS

### Creating Crops

By choosing seeds from plants that need less water, scientists are producing strains of crops that can better survive droughts. A science research institute in Karnal, India, has already developed wheat and rice that can tolerate droughts. Other scientists are experimenting with plant genes to understand plant growth and survival, in order to produce crops that can resist drought.

CHAPTER THREE

# Ecosystems in Turmoil

The world's climates have changed many times in the past. At one time, much of Earth was hotter and wetter than it is today, and during periods known as ice ages, it was much colder. Most plants and animals can adapt to changes in climate, provided they have enough time. The problem with today's climate change is that it is happening so fast that most species are struggling to adapt.

## Vulnerable Ecosystems

An ecosystem consists of all the plants and animals that rely on each other for survival in a particular habitat. Plants make their own food through photosynthesis, but animals survive directly or indirectly on plants. Many plants rely on insects and other animals to pollinate their flowers. The entire ecosystem needs scavengers and decomposers to break up plant and animal remains and return the nutrients to the soil.

Many animals are found in only one part of the world. This particular red tree frog lives in tropical rain forests in South America.

# ECOSYSTEMS IN TURMOIL

## Safe Habitats

The plants and animals in an ecosystem have developed special ways of dealing with their particular habitat. For example, many desert plants store water in their leaves or stems. Desert animals lose very little water, and many hide from the scorching heat by living in tunnels underground. These adaptations have evolved over many thousands or millions of years.

## Threats to Ecosystems

Ecosystems are under threat from two sources: climate change and population growth. Climate change may alter the actual habitat. For example, droughts change semidesert into desert, where existing plants and animals can no longer survive. As the human population grows, people take over natural habitats to create more farms and to build factories, towns, and roads.

Food is scarce in a desert, but some woodpeckers feed on cactus fruits and insects, including insects that visit the cactus flowers.

### LOOK TO THE PAST

A huge change in climate occurred 56 million years ago. The average temperature of Earth rose by 11°F (6°C), but this change took around 20,000 years. The oceans became much warmer and reached about 95°F (35°C) near the equator. As a result, a vast number of deep-sea creatures became extinct.

# THE RACE TO SURVIVE CLIMATE CHANGE

## Adapt or Move

How can plants and animals survive when their habitat changes? If they cannot adapt to the new situation, they must move to a new habitat that better suits them. American pikas live on high, cold mountainsides. As their homes become too warm, they move higher up the mountain—until they run out of mountain. Other species are moving into habitats that were previously too cold for them. The newcomers can cause problems for plants and animals that already live there.

## Wildlife Invasions

Cooler lands, forests, and rivers are all being invaded. As the Arctic becomes warmer, forest trees are growing farther north and taking over some of the tundra. This leaves less space for tundra animals, such as caribou and Arctic foxes. Forests of spruce and fir are also losing ground to trees from the south, such as maple, beech, oak, and hickory. Trout and salmon like cold water, but as their rivers become warmer, they are losing their habitats to incoming fish.

Arctic foxes live on the tundra. Climate change is making life more difficult for them. Their territory is being invaded by red foxes and by forest trees.

ECOSYSTEMS IN TURMOIL

## Bad Timing

Species that remain where they are may face other problems. As spring comes earlier, some plants and trees are blooming earlier, too. If they rely on insects to pollinate their flowers, however, they could be in trouble. By the time the insects emerge and search for pollen, the flowers may have died. Ducks, geese, and other birds fly toward the polar regions to produce young. They are arriving in their breeding grounds earlier than before, but sometimes too early to find food.

Baobab trees can survive short droughts. Climate change, however, is threatening the only habitats of three of the nine types of baobab.

## COUNTDOWN!

One-third of Peru's different species of birds, frogs, and mammals live in forests on the steep sides of the Andes Mountains. In the past, when the climate has changed, the trees and the animals have gradually moved up or down the mountainside. According to researchers at Wake Forest University in North Carolina, the climate is now changing so quickly that this unique ecosystem could be wiped out by 2100.

THE RACE TO SURVIVE CLIMATE CHANGE

## In the Oceans

The oceans cover nearly three-quarters of Earth's surface. According to the IPCC, the oceans have absorbed more than 90 percent of the heat generated by excess greenhouse gases since 1971. They have also absorbed about 30 percent of the carbon dioxide produced by humans. The carbon dioxide, however, is making seawater more acidic.

## Seawater Acid Attack

Carbon dioxide from the atmosphere reacts with seawater to produce carbonic acid. This is making life particularly difficult for crustaceans, a large group of animals that includes shrimps, lobsters, squid, and the tiny polyps that build coral reefs. The acid makes it harder for crustaceans to build their shells. It particularly affects small crustaceans, such as krill and the pteropod, one of the microscopic animals that form plankton, a vital source of food for many sea creatures.

▲ A lobster's body and legs are protected by hard shells. As lobsters grow, they make new shells and shed the old ones.

24

## Coral Reefs

Because they support more different species than any other ocean habitat, coral reefs are vital to the health of the seas. However, coral reefs are affected not only by increasing acidity, but also by warmer ocean temperatures. When ocean temperatures rise more than a few degrees, the coral polyps lose their color and may die. According to the International Union for Conservation of Nature (IUCN), about 20 percent of the world's coral reefs have been damaged beyond repair. This already serious situation is only likely to get worse as the oceans warm further.

### SCIENCE SOLUTIONS

## Vital Plankton

The microscopic plants in plankton are crucial to life on Earth. According to a scientist at the National Oceanography Centre (NOC) in Southampton, England, plankton produces about half of the oxygen in the air that we breathe. It also removes carbon dioxide. Although these plants are too small to see with the naked eye, satellites in space can detect them as mass patches of green that show up on satellite photos of the oceans. This allows scientists to monitor how plankton changes over the year and where it is most abundant.

Coral reefs surround many tropical islands. The reefs protect the shore from storms. Coral reefs are dying due to the sea becoming too warm and too acidic.

25

# THE RACE TO SURVIVE CLIMATE CHANGE

## Extinction of Species

The IPCC estimates that if Earth's temperature rises by more than 2.7°F to 4.5°F (1.5°C to 2.5°C), between 20 and 30 percent of plant and animal species could become extinct. The species most at risk are not only those that cannot survive the hotter temperatures, but also species that have been disrupted by changes to their food chains and habitats caused by climate change. Animals at risk include polar bears, clouded leopards, leatherback sea turtles, and some penguins.

## Rising Temperatures

Leatherback turtles spend most of their lives at sea, but the females crawl up beaches to lay their eggs and bury them in the sand. The gender of the baby turtle depends on the temperature of the sand. Warmer temperatures produce more females. According to the environmental organization Conservation International, if turtles cannot find cooler beaches, there could in the future be no males to ensure the survival of the species.

Emperor penguins lay their eggs and raise their chicks on thick ice shelves. Parts of these ice shelves are disappearing, putting the penguins at risk.

ECOSYSTEMS IN TURMOIL

## Changing Habitats

A polar bear's main source of food is seals. The bears hunt seals by waiting on the Arctic sea ice for their prey to come to the surface to breathe in air. In summer, the ice melts and it becomes much more difficult for the bears to catch seals. Because of climate change, sea ice is now melting earlier and freezing later. Polar bears are already dying from starvation during the ice-free months of summer. As this trend continues, they could become extinct.

Polar bear cubs are born in spring. This gives the mother just a short time to catch seals for herself and her cubs before the ice melts.

### LOOK TO THE PAST

When Earth warmed by about 11°F (6°C) about 56 million years ago, the rise in temperature occurred at the same time as a huge increase in carbon dioxide in the atmosphere. Scientists at the Scripps Institution of Oceanography in California want to use that period as a model for what might happen now. The rise in temperature is similar to that predicted for 2100 if global warming continues at its present rate. Long ago, the warm period lasted 200,000 years, so a similar change today could go on for just as long, leading to the extinction of millions of species.

CHAPTER FOUR

# Melting Ice

Antarctica and the Arctic are the coldest, iciest places on Earth, but they are warming faster than anywhere else. According to the NASA Earth Observatory, from 2000 to 2009 the land temperatures in the Arctic and the Antarctic Peninsula (the northernmost part of Antarctica) increased three to four times more than ocean temperatures. Warmer temperatures have led to more ice melting in the sea and from glaciers on land, particularly in the Arctic.

## Glaciers on the Move

Glaciers are frozen sheets of freshwater ice. Antarctica is covered by an ice cap that is several miles thick. The largest glacier in the Northern Hemisphere covers the island of Greenland. Glaciers in Antarctica and the Arctic move slowly downhill toward the sea. When they reach the ocean, large chunks break off and float away as icebergs. As the temperature rises, glaciers are melting and moving faster. As a result, more and more freshwater is now pouring into the world's oceans.

In 2002, the massive Larsen B ice shelf collapsed and split into many icebergs. The ice shelf was about the same area as the state of Rhode Island.

# MELTING ICE

## Melting Mountain Glaciers

High mountaintops are also covered by glaciers. The lower extremities of these glaciers melt and retreat in summer and refreeze in winter. Warmer temperatures mean that the glaciers are melting further and refreezing less. The extra water created by the melting glaciers pours into rivers and eventually into the sea.

## Rising Seas

As the oceans become warmer, they expand. This, together with the melted freshwater, has caused the level of the sea to rise. NASA satellites have shown that sea levels since 2000 have risen faster than they did between 1870 and 2000. Even a small rise in the surface of the oceans causes increased flooding along low-lying coasts.

### COUNTDOWN!

According to the NASA Earth Observatory, the surface of the sea rose by 1.89 inches (4.8 centimeters) between 1993 and 2009. The IPCC estimates that the sea will continue to rise 0.59–1.9 feet (0.18–0.59 meters) by 2099. This prediction does not take into account the extra water from melting glaciers, so the actual rise is likely to be much greater.

During the last ice age, Norway was an area of mountains on the edge of a plain. When the ice melted, sea flooded the plain and valleys.

# THE RACE TO SURVIVE CLIMATE CHANGE

## Arctic Meltdown

The Arctic is feeling the heat. The ice that covers the Arctic Ocean is becoming thinner, and more of it is melting during summer. The land around the Arctic Ocean—the permafrost—is melting. The Inuit people who live near the Arctic Ocean, and the wildlife that lives there, particularly polar bears, are losing their homes and habitats. Meanwhile, oil companies are moving in, looking for rich reserves beneath the ice.

## Less Ice, More Sea

Some of the Arctic sea ice naturally melts in summer and refreezes in winter. Climate change is causing much more ice to melt. This, too, is having an effect on climate change. According to the NASA Earth Observatory, about 270,000 square miles (700,000 square kilometers) more ice disappeared in 2012 than in 2007. The more ice melts, the more sea is exposed. White ice reflects the sun's energy, but dark water absorbs it, adding to global warming.

> The geographic North Pole is in the Arctic Ocean. It has been thick ice for thousands of years, but could soon become open ocean.

# MELTING ICE

Much of America's oil is drilled in northern Alaska. Oil companies now want to drill for even more oil along the edge of the Arctic Ocean.

## New Opportunities

The shrinking ice cap over the Arctic Ocean has opened up new possibilities for shipping companies and oil companies. In summer, it is now possible for ships to sail around the north of Canada and Alaska, creating a shortcut between the Atlantic and Pacific Oceans. Oil companies know that there is oil below the Arctic seabed and are eager to start drilling.

## Making Matters Worse

Conservationist groups, such as Greenpeace, are fiercely opposed to exploiting the Arctic Ocean. They point out that an oil spill would cause catastrophic damage to wildlife, and that the oil obtained would increase greenhouse gases and global warming.

### COUNTDOWN!

How long will it be before the Arctic Ocean is completely ice-free in summer? Following the big sea-ice melt of 2007, the British Met Office predicted that the first ice-free summer would not occur before 2060 or 2080. However, in 2013 scientists from NOAA predicted that the Arctic would be nearly ice-free much sooner than first predicted—sometime between 2020 and 2060.

# THE RACE TO SURVIVE CLIMATE CHANGE

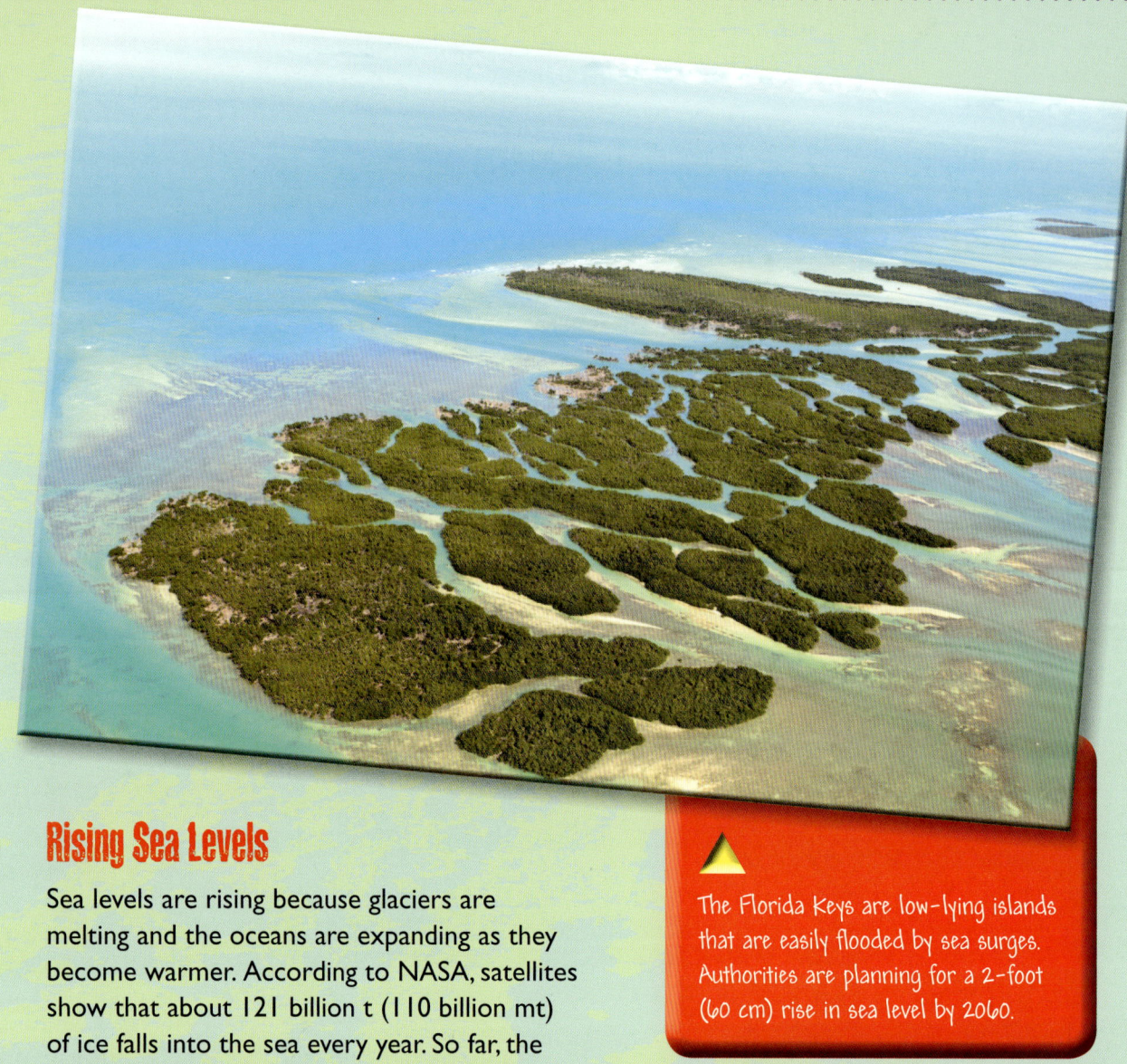

## Rising Sea Levels

Sea levels are rising because glaciers are melting and the oceans are expanding as they become warmer. According to NASA, satellites show that about 121 billion t (110 billion mt) of ice falls into the sea every year. So far, the rise in sea level is small, but even this rise is already damaging beaches and coasts.

The Florida Keys are low-lying islands that are easily flooded by sea surges. Authorities are planning for a 2-foot (60 cm) rise in sea level by 2060.

## Low-Lying Coasts

According to the NASA Earth Observatory, 10 percent of the world's people live in areas less than 33 ft (10 m) above sea level. Some islands in the Pacific Ocean, such as Tuvalu, and the Maldives in the Indian Ocean are particularly at risk, because none of the land is more than a few feet above sea level. The NASA Earth Observatory predicts that many islands will disappear below the rising waves.

MELTING ICE

## Changing Shorelines

In some places, rising sea levels are washing away, or eroding, beaches and coastlines. The Eastern Seaboard is being eroded by storms, rising sea levels, and human activities. According to researchers at the University of Virginia, the Atlantic coast is eroding by 2–3 ft (0.6–0.9 m) each year. Part of the Louisiana coastline, however, is eroding by an astounding 50 ft (15 m) a year.

**LOOK TO THE PAST**

About 21,000 years ago, during the last ice age, Earth's average temperature was around 9°F (5°C) lower than it is now. So much water was locked up in ice that the level of the sea was 400 ft (122 m) lower than it is today. North America was connected to Asia by a land bridge, and Britain was connected to the rest of Europe. As Earth gradually warmed, the ice melted and the sea level rose, flooding the land bridge and forming the North Sea between Britain and continental Europe. The IPCC predicts that there could be a similar rise in temperature by 2100.

Tuvalu is a narrow strip of coral islands around a large lagoon. The highest point is just 13 ft (4 m) above sea level, but most of the islands are lower.

33

# THE RACE TO SURVIVE CLIMATE CHANGE

## Coastal Floods

Floods caused by climate change threaten low-lying coasts around the world. Rising sea levels, storm waves, and melting mountain glaciers all lead to catastrophic floods. Huge areas of coast are at risk, particularly around the mouths of large rivers such as the Mississippi in North America, and the Ganges and the Mekong in Asia.

## Too Much Water

Hurricanes create storm surges in which the level of the sea rises several feet higher than usual. When a hurricane reaches land, the storm surge and huge waves whipped up by the winds crash over the shore, flooding homes, cities, and farmland. Water from melting glaciers and storms pour into rivers. Much of the Asian country of Bangladesh is low-lying and constantly threatened by floods from the sea and the Ganges River.

Zeeland in the Netherlands is protected from storms by a 1.9-mile (3 km) long movable barrier. The barrier is closed when a storm is forecast.

# MELTING ICE

## Holding Back the Sea

In some places, a seawall is built to stop the waves flooding onto the land. For example, Malé, the main island of the Maldives, is encircled by a massive seawall. Much of New Orleans is actually below sea level, and so the city is protected by levees, or floodwalls. In 2005, however, the levees broke when Hurricane Katrina hit, and New Orleans was flooded.

## Leaving the Coast

According to the NRC, if the sea level rises by 20 in (50 cm), up to 200 million people who live on the coast could be affected. Up to 4 million people would have to leave their homes and live elsewhere. Where would all of these people go? Many countries, such as Bangladesh, have no space inland for people to live.

## SCIENCE SOLUTIONS

### Flood Protection

The Dutch have experienced many floods. About two-thirds of the Netherlands is at risk for flooding, but dams, dykes (levees), and floodgates protect the land. Dutch engineers have recently built a new kind of flood protection, called the Zandmotor, or Sand Motor. It is a vast heap of sand and sediment that has been dumped along a stretch of coast. Ocean currents will gradually move the sand along the coast and so protect it from erosion.

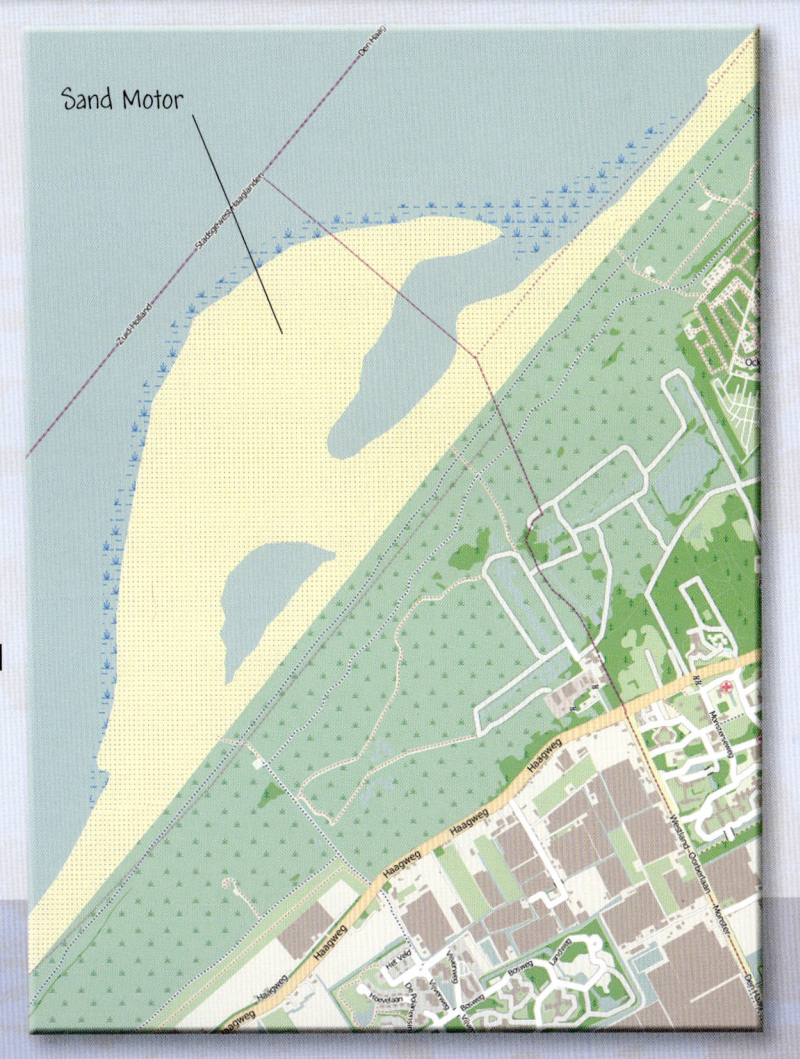

CHAPTER FIVE

# Cutting the Carbon

Climate change threatens our ability to survive on Earth. Disappearing coastlines, floods, droughts, and failed crops are already occurring. In 2013, the IPCC reported that its scientists are now 97 percent sure that, since the 1950s, humans have been mainly responsible for the carbon dioxide and other greenhouses gases that have produced climate change.

## Avoiding the Worst

Carbon that is already in the atmosphere will stay there for centuries, so we cannot escape its impact. It will continue to warm the planet long after 2100. The more carbon and greenhouse gases we emit, the higher the temperature will rise. Can we avoid the worst consequences of climate change by limiting the rise in Earth's temperature to 3.6°F (2°C) or less?

Many existing factories produce tons of greenhouse gases and air pollution. New technology is needed to make factories much cleaner.

## Cutting Carbon

According to the NRC, the amount of carbon in the atmosphere is now higher than at any time in the last 800,000 years. The only way humans can dramatically reduce carbon emissions is to stop burning fossil fuels and stop cutting down forests.

## Counting the Cost

We already have ways of producing energy without burning fossil fuels, and scientists and engineers are continually coming up with new ideas. The question is whether governments will invest in these new ideas. The Dutch Sand Motor, for example, cost $67 million, but this is only about half the cost of repairing coastal erosion. In 2006, the British economist Nicholas Stern released an important report, called the *Stern Review*, which showed that it is far cheaper to avoid the impact of climate change than to pay for the consequences.

◀ Air pollution causes smog, which is very unhealthy. In some cities the pollution is so severe that people protect themselves by wearing face masks.

## COUNTDOWN!

To stop Earth's temperature rising more than 3.6°F (2°C), the IPCC advises that humans must not allow their total carbon emissions go above 800 billion t (726 billion mt) of carbon. We have already added about 531 billions t (482 billion mt) to the atmosphere, so we are already two-thirds of the way to the total.

# THE RACE TO SURVIVE CLIMATE CHANGE

## Tackling Transportation

Most automobiles, trucks, ships, and aircraft burn fuel made from oil. According to the EPA, transportation created 31 percent of the United States' carbon emissions between 1990 and 2011. By that last date, transportation was adding more than 1,923 million t (1,745 million mt) of carbon dioxide to the atmosphere every year. What can be done to cut these enormous emissions?

## New Fuels

One way to cut emissions is to find alternative, cleaner fuels. Biofuel made from plants is one type of alternative fuel. It can be mixed with gasoline and used in most motor vehicles. In the United States, biofuel is made mainly from corn. This means, however, that land that was previously used to grow crops for food is now being used instead to grow plants for fuel, which makes food scarcer and more expensive, causing an increasing problem worldwide.

Some cities have so many cars that traffic backs up even on multilane highways. Cars with engines that switch off automatically when the cars are not moving help prevent pollution.

Electric cars are cheap to run and will become more common as recharging stations are made more available.

## Electric Motors

Car manufacturers are now making cars that run on electricity. Electric cars produce no exhaust fumes that pollute the air, but do they cut carbon emissions? The answer depends on how the electricity is produced. If the electricity is generated by burning fossil fuels, then electric cars are still adding carbon to Earth's atmosphere.

## Clean Fuel

Hydrogen is the cleanest fuel for transportation. Instead of burning it, people can use it in a type of battery called a hydrogen fuel cell, which produces electricity to power the electric motor. In a small number of cities, such as London and Reykjavik, some buses already use fuel cells, but they are still far too expensive for general use.

## SCIENCE SOLUTIONS

### Efficient Cars

One way to reduce carbon is to make vehicles more efficient. Designers and engineers are making good progress in increasing the number of miles a vehicle can travel on a gallon of fuel. A hybrid is a vehicle that uses a small gasoline engine and an electric motor. The latest hybrids can achieve 300 miles per gallon (100 kilometers per liter).

The wind at sea is generally more reliable than on land. Offshore wind turbines are larger than onshore turbines and generate more electricity, more reliably.

## Essential Electricity

In the United States, 38 percent of carbon emissions are produced by power stations that burn coal, oil, or natural gas to generate electricity. World demand for electricity is increasing, so it is urgent that the United States and other countries switch to methods of generating electricity that do not produce huge amounts of carbon.

## Clean Alternatives

There are already many ways of generating electricity that produce little or no carbon. They include hydroelectricity (generated by the force of moving water), wind turbines, and solar power. Earth receives enough energy from the sun every minute to provide all the energy we need for a year. Solar panels and solar power stations already convert some of this energy into electricity, but so far they convert only a tiny fraction of the energy that is available from the sun.

## Awesome Electricity

Electricity is incredibly useful and adaptable. Americans and people around the world rely on electricity to power lights, computers, factory machines, and a vast range of equipment and gadgets. Small gadgets, such as cell phones, tablets, and flashlights, run on electricity generated in a battery.

CUTTING THE CARBON

## Increasing Demand

Not only are gadgets that use electricity increasingly available, there are also now many more people who use them. As countries with big populations, such as Brazil and India, become wealthier, the people who live there demand more electricity. The Internet, for example, with its browsers and huge data storage facilities, consumes ever-increasing amounts of electricity around the world.

Some of the electrical energy that leaves a power station is lost as it is transmitted along cables. Using many thin wires is even more wasteful.

### SCIENCE SOLUTIONS

## Ambitious Projects

Engineers at the Institution of Mechanical Engineers in London say that humans cannot limit the consequences of climate change without the help of large, ambitious projects. These include setting up forests of "artificial trees" to absorb carbon dioxide from the air, and mirrors to reflect sunlight back into space. Both of these projects are very expensive, however, and may take so long to set up that they will not be ready in time to halt climate change.

41

## THE RACE TO SURVIVE CLIMATE CHANGE

## Saving Energy

Along with generating electricity without increasing carbon emissions, we need to consume less energy of all types. Many motor vehicles already travel farther on less fuel, but drivers of those vehicles can take action to save fuel, too. There are also many ways to save energy at home, including insulation and more efficient machines and gadgets.

## Saving Gasoline

The best way to save gasoline is to leave the car at home, and bicycle or walk wherever possible. Sharing rides and using buses or trains also helps. When driving, people can save gasoline using simple measures such as driving at a moderate, steady speed instead of constantly accelerating and braking, and checking tires to make sure they are at the correct pressure.

## Being More Efficient

Manufacturers are now producing gadgets that use less electricity. The "eco" setting on a dishwasher or washing machine may take longer to complete its cycle, but it uses less water and less energy. People can be more efficient, too. There are many ways to save electricity, including turning lights off when leaving a room and not leaving televisions, laptops, and other devices on standby.

The color green, leaves, and the word "eco" are often used to show that something is designed to reduce carbon emissions.

CUTTING THE CARBON

## Insulating the Home

Insulation is an additional layer in the outer walls, roof, and sometimes the floor of a building. The extra layer keeps heat in when it is cold outside, and keeps the inside cooler in summer. A building that is well insulated and has double- or triple-glazed windows uses only a fraction of the energy used by an uninsulated building.

The Hearst Tower is a tall office building in New York. It was designed to use 26 percent less energy and 20 percent less steel than most other skyscrapers.

### LOOK TO THE PAST

One way to save energy and money is to use old-fashioned, low-tech ways of doing things. Traditional building materials, such as wood and adobe, are much better insulators than the concrete, glass, and steel often used today. The design of buildings is important, too. For example, most homes in very hot countries in North Africa were traditionally built around shady, cool courtyards.

# THE RACE TO SURVIVE CLIMATE CHANGE

*A severe drought leaves the soil too cracked and hard for crops to grow. Can we prevent this becoming a common sight in many countries in future?*

## Can We Win the Race?

Can humans cut enough carbon from their emissions to avoid the worst consequences of climate change? They can, but only if the world's governments and peoples are determined to take action and work together. They have made a start, but they need to do much more—and fast. However, a powerful group of people known as "climate skeptics" continually resists efforts to tackle climate change.

## Denying Climate Change

At first, climate skeptics denied that Earth is warming, and then, when the evidence was undeniable, they said climate change was due to natural causes, not human activities. Climate skeptics want to continue burning more and more fossil fuels.

## The Consequences of Doing Nothing

If we continue to produce greenhouse gases at the rate we currently are, the IPCC predicts that Earth's temperature will rise by up to 8.6°F (4.8°C) by 2100, and sea levels will rise by as much as 1.9 ft (0.59 m). According to the NASA Earth Observatory, the rise could actually be double when water from melting glaciers is added. If NASA is correct, coastal flooding will cause serious devastation to many people in many parts of the world.

## CUTTING THE CARBON

### Surviving Climate Change

Winning the race for survival against climate change means limiting the rise in temperature to 3.6°F (2°C). If we lose the race against climate change, low-lying cities, islands, and coasts will be flooded, millions of species will become extinct, and famine and extreme weather will become even more severe.

### COUNTDOWN!

The concentration of carbon in the atmosphere is measured as parts per million (ppm). The NRC has reported that in the 200 years up to 2010, the concentration of carbon in the air increased from about 280 ppm to 390 ppm. If we do nothing, the concentration of carbon will rise to almost 900 ppm by 2100. To stop the concentration from increasing, we need to reduce global carbon emissions by 80 percent.

People dressed as pandas and 100,000 other protesters urged governments attending a UN Climate Change Conference to take action to reduce carbon emissions.

45

# Glossary

**ecologist** A scientist who studies the relationship between living things and their environment.

**ecosystem** All the living and nonliving things that make up a habitat.

**emission** The release of a gas into the atmosphere.

**Environmental Protection Agency (EPA)** A U.S. government agency set up to protect the environment and the health of the American people.

**genes** Complex parts of a living cell that are inherited from parents and control what each living cell does.

**glacier** A large mass of land ice.

**global warming** An increase in the average temperature of the surface of Earth.

**hybrid** An automobile that is powered by a small gasoline engine linked to an electric motor.

**ice age** A long period in the past during which thick ice sheets covered vast areas of land.

**ice core** A tube of ice taken from a glacier in order to gain information about climate patterns and the atmosphere in the past.

**insulation** The use of materials to stop heat from moving from one space to another.

**Intergovernmental Panel on Climate Change (IPCC)** The leading international organization for assessing climate change.

**meteorologist** A scientist who studies and predicts the weather.

**methane** One of the gases in the air that increases global warming.

**National Aeronautics and Space Administration (NASA)** The organization in charge of the U.S. space program.

**National Oceanic and Atmospheric Administration (NOAA)** The U.S. government agency for the oceans and atmosphere.

**National Research Council (NRC)** An organization in the U.S. that reports on scientific, engineering, and health matters.

**parts per million (ppm)** A way of measuring the concentration of gases.

**permafrost** Land beneath the surface of the soil that is permanently frozen.

**photosynthesis** The process by which plants use the energy of sunlight to combine water with carbon dioxide to make plant sugar.

**plankton** Microscopic plants and animals that form the basis of almost all ocean food chains.

**pollinate** The transfer of pollen from one plant to another plant of the same type.

**species** A group of living things that are similar and can mate and produce young.

**storm surge** A temporary rise in the level of the ocean associated with a hurricane.

**yield** The weight of grain produced by a cereal crop per acre (or hectare) of land.

# Further Reading

## Books

Kaye, Cathryn Berger. *A Kid's Guide to Climate Change & Global Warming: (How to Take Action!)*. Minneapolis, MN: Free Spirit Publishing, 2009.

Cherry, Lynne, and Gary Braasch. *How We Know What We Know About Our Changing Climate: Scientists and Kids Explore Global Warming*. Nevada City, CA: Dawn Publications, 2010.

Dorion, Christiane. *How the Weather Works: A Hands-on Guide to Our Changing Climate* (Explore the Earth). Dorking, UK: Templar, 2011.

Henson, Robert. *The Rough Guide to Climate Change* (Rough Guides). London, UK: Rough Guides, 2011.

Pollack, Henry. *A World Without Ice*. New York, NY: Penguin, 2009.

Simpson, Kathleen. *Extreme Weather: Science Tackles Global Warming and Climate Change* (National Geographic Investigates). Des Moines, IA: National Geographic Children's Books, 2008.

Woodward, John. *Climate Change* (Eyewitness Books). New York, NY: Dorling Kindersley, 2008.

## Web Sites

Due to the changing nature of Internet links, Rosen Publishing has developed an online list of Web sites related to the subject of this book. This site is updated regularly. Please use this link to access the list:

http://www.rosenlinks.com/WIC/Clim

# Index

acidity 24, 25
Africa 18, 43
agriculture 16, 18–19, 36, 38
air pollution 36, 37
aircraft 9
Antarctica 7, 28
Arctic 10, 22, 27, 28, 30–31
Arctic foxes 22
Australia 13

Bangladesh 34, 35
baobab trees 23
bark beetles 19
biofuel 38
building design 43

Canada 14, 17, 31
carbon 9, 11, 36, 37, 39, 45
carbon dioxide 7, 9, 10, 11, 24, 25, 27, 36, 38, 41
carbon emissions 7, 9, 37, 38, 39, 40, 42, 44, 45
cars 38, 39, 42
coal 8, 9, 40
coastal erosion 33, 37
Colorado potato beetles 19
coral reefs 24, 25
crustaceans 24

deforestation 11, 19, 37
deserts 21
droughts 12, 16, 18, 19, 21, 23, 36, 44

ecosystems, threats to 20–27
electricity 8, 9, 39, 40–41
emperor penguins 26
energy efficiency 42–43
extinctions 4, 21, 26, 27, 45
extreme weather 5, 12–19, 34–35, 45

flooding 12, 13, 16–17, 29, 32, 33, 34–35, 36, 44, 45

Florida Keys 32
fossil fuels 8, 9, 37, 39, 44
fuel efficiency 39, 42

glaciers 28, 29, 32, 34, 44
global warming 5, 6, 9, 10, 11, 12, 17, 26, 27, 28, 30, 31, 33, 44
greenhouse gases 7, 8, 9, 10, 24, 31, 36, 44

heat waves 12, 19
hurricanes 12, 14–15, 32, 34, 35
hybrid vehicles 39
hydroelectricity 40
hydrogen fuel cells 39

ice ages 5, 6, 20, 29, 33
ice, melting 7, 10, 11, 12, 26, 27, 28–31, 32, 44
India 18, 19, 41
Industrial Revolution 8, 9
insulation 43
Intergovernmental Panel on Climate Change (IPCC) 4, 6, 7, 8, 12, 16, 24, 26, 29, 33, 36, 37, 44
Inuit 30

Larsen B ice shelf 28
leatherback turtles 26
lobsters 24

Maldives 32, 35
Mediterranean 4
meteorologists 4, 12, 13, 15
methane 7, 9, 10
migrations 5, 23
mountains 22, 23, 29

natural gas 8, 9, 40
Netherlands 34, 35
nitrous oxide 10
North Pole 30
Norway 29

oceans 21, 24–25, 28, 29, 30–31, 32
oil 8, 9, 30, 31, 38, 40
oxygen 25

permafrost 10, 30
pests, plant 19
Philippines 15
pikas 22
plankton 24, 25
polar bears 26, 27, 30
pollination 20, 23
population growth 21

rainstorms 12, 16, 17

science and technology 9, 15, 19, 35, 37, 38–43
sea ice 11, 27, 30–31
sea levels, rising 5, 29, 32–33, 34, 35, 44
solar power 6, 30, 40
South America 20, 23, 41
steam power 8
storm surges 32, 34
storms 12, 14–15

temperature, Earth's 4, 5, 6, 7, 8, 18, 21, 26, 27, 28, 33, 36, 37, 44, 45
tornadoes 12, 14
transportation 9, 38–39, 42
tree frogs 20
tundra 10, 22
Tuvalu 32, 33
Typhoon Halyan 15

United States 12–13, 14, 16, 17, 18, 19, 32, 33, 34, 35, 38, 40, 43

water vapor 6, 7, 16
wildfires 11, 16
wildlife 5, 10, 20–27, 30, 31
wind turbines 40

48